THE GRATITUDE
CONNECTION

Amy Collette

embrace the positive power of thanks

A Wild Grace Publishing Publication
All rights reserved

Copyright © 2015 by Amy Collette (AmyCollette.com)

Published and distributed in the United States by:
Wild Grace Publishing
PO Box 270098
Louisville, CO 80027
wildgracepublishing.com

Project Editor: Ken Chartrand
Cover Design: Rebecca Lefebvre, Reda Creative
Interior Design: Rebecca Lefebvre, Reda Creative
Author Photo: Laurie Feauto

Collette, Amy
The Gratitude Connection: Embrace the positive powerful thanks
ISBN: 978-0-9961692-0-2

2nd edition, April 2015
First published November, 2012

Grateful Acknowledgments

With great delight, I thank everyone who has been a part of bringing this second edition of *The Gratitude Connection* to the world. My heart is bursting with gratitude for your wisdom, love, support, and guidance:

Thank you, Tom, my love and greatest supporter and teacher. You teach me what it means to live with a happy, loving, and compassionate heart. You have shown me more love than I thought was possible.

Thanks from my heart to my family for the things that matter most: love, laughter, creativity, strength, integrity, nature, music, and dance. To my sister-in-law Rochelle and the whole Casey family, thank you for making me one of your own.

Deep thanks to the friends who are my circle of light, for sharing your love and enthusiasm (as well as your listening and editing skills) to make this dream come true. Thanks from my heart to Jenny Blanchard, Laurie Feauto, Betsy Gillis, Kelly Ballard, Joan and Spencer Guthrie, Deb and Charlie Dillon, Marilee and Rupert Ross, Diane and Wendell King, the Pinecliffe community, Roger House, Stephanie Flanders-Martin, G. and Bridget Brown, David Doroski, Fr. Bob Konopa, Doug Edmundson, Davis Phinney, Connie Carpenter Phinney, Carl Ames and family, Joe and Jan Williams, the Davis Phinney Foundation,

Kisa Harris and my YMCA friends, Lynn Scheurell and the Catalyst Mastermind group, and all the friends, mentors, and clients who have shared their hearts with me.

Thank you Rebecca Lefebvre, for creating the beautiful look and feel of the book, along with your love and encouragement. Special thanks to my editor Ken Chartrand for being the champion of my readers and making me a better writer.

You are all angels on earth. I am lifted up by your love and support. May you be abundantly blessed as I have been blessed by you.

Dedication

To Tom, whose love lights my way

Table of Contents

Introduction: It Starts with a Spark

Gratitude is a powerful catalyst for happiness.
It's the spark that lights a fire of joy in your soul.
~ Amy Collette

Are you one of those people who wakes up cheery every morning? Do you bound out of bed feeling great and looking forward to the day? If you are, congratulations! You have a head start on *The Gratitude Connection*. If you're not, don't worry. I wasn't either.

Can you even imagine what it would be like to go to bed feeling happy about the day you just had, and looking forward to tomorrow? As impossible as that might feel right now, you could be one of those happy people, too.

I can only say that with confidence because I used to be a big grump in the morning. I woke up full of anxiety about the day and unhappy about having to get up. I thought that was "just the way I was" and I couldn't change it. I believed this even though I lived with one of the most positive people on the planet: my husband, Tom.

Then I started practicing gratitude. I spent a few minutes focusing on gratitude when I went to bed, and again when I woke up in the morning. I was just trying to feel better, to feel a little less stress and anxiety. A few days into this new habit, a weird thing happened. I started to look forward to waking up. I couldn't wait for those few minutes of thanks in the morning when I felt at peace; calm and grounded.

It was only another week or so that other people started to notice a change in me. I finally understood Tom's cheerful outlook. I had found a spark of happiness and kept it burning by practicing gratitude every day.

One simple new habit made all these profound changes. It made me see that my essential self, the love and positivity within me, had been hidden. It took letting myself feel gratitude to let the light inside shine through so I could see it. When I saw it in myself, it was easy to see it in everyone around me — even if they were grumpy on the outside...

When you let yourself shine, you become a magnet for other people who shine the same way. I started discussing gratitude with other people, and they shared their own experiences of gratitude and healing.

And that's how *The Gratitude Connection* was born. I gathered the stories together as a guide for a joyous life.

Gratitude helps connect us to Spirit, the light that connects us to ourselves and each other. It helps us celebrate the good times and sustains us through the sad ones.

At any time, you can find one thing that's going well in your life. It might not be perfect, but it's there — even if it's just a spark. If you're really depressed, you might think that nothing in your life is great. But even when you're very down or anxious, take a deep breath and just listen. Listen for that one thing that's going well for you. Do you have enough to eat? Do you have one relationship that you can turn to? Do you have a job? Do you have enough money to pay your bills? How about a companion who loves you? Is there a point in your week that gives you some satisfaction or insight or connection — like at church or during meditation? Does your body (or any part of it) feel strong and healthy?

Really look for a part that is flowing easily, that you might be taking for granted. You may come up with many more than one, but one is all you need to start with.

That's the spark that can start a fire in your life. The spark that you can build on. When you recognize that spark, concentrate on it and let it help connect you to gratitude. Let that positive power illuminate other parts of your life.

Feel free to take your time as you read through *The Gratitude Connection*. This book is not necessarily meant to be read cover to cover in one sitting. Read one section at a time and work through the practices. Discover which new habits work for you and make them your own. Sharing the book and your experiences with it helps you deepen your own connection to gratitude. I invite you to share it with your friends and family, or start a Gratitude Connection Circle with a group of people to work through the book together.

May you be blessed with the positive power of gratitude.
~ Amy Collette

Practicing Gratitude

Gratitude is not only the greatest of virtues,
but the parent of all others.
~Cicero

I'm a lucky person. Most of my life I have had an easy time getting good grades or landing a job or starting a business. The most stressful times were when someone I loved was sick or struggling. I have felt since I was a kid that I lived a charmed life.

But a few years ago, I experienced what I call my own personal recession. Since my consulting business was consistent and busy, I wasn't spending much time or energy marketing new business. Then suddenly, one of my two major clients ran out of funding and closed his business. Two weeks later, my other big client company was sold. They no longer needed me.

My husband also had his own business. Over the years, when one of our businesses hit a slump, the other business was strong, so we were always able to ride the waves of economic change. This was the first time we both hit a slump at the same time. And it was a pretty big slump.

With a big mortgage and lots of debt, it wasn't long until we were borrowing money to pay the bills and using credit cards to buy groceries. It made me crazy.

I didn't expect to be at such a desperate place at that stage of my life, when things had been so comfortable. But there I was. I had a hard time sleeping, and I'd wake up with my heart pounding, my head spinning with pictures of losing our house.

Then I read about a Jewish tradition of practicing gratitude. Hakarat hatov (recognizing the good) is reciting a prayer of gratitude several times a day so that it becomes part of your routine, a habit. I liked the idea, but how could I be grateful for anything? It felt like everything was going wrong.

But I began. In the morning I gave thanks for health, for my husband, for a roof over my head, for the deep love and friendships in my life. At night I focused on gratitude for everything I had learned during the day.

I'll admit that at first it was a chore. I made myself do it, and sometimes I faked it. But I kept at it.

Then I noticed a subtle shift in my attitude. I was finding more things to be grateful for. A sunrise. A conversation with an old friend. Time with my old dog. Reconciliation with family. A bigger picture beyond my immediate problems began to take over my perspective. I started to see solutions to our problems, such as selling the house, and finding work in a different industry. We had options, but most of all, I was feeling a sense of security, a sense that I would always be OK. I started to experience a spiritual connection more and more, especially when I was out in nature.

That was when I started to sleep again. I could see that my life was full. What I worried about was a possible future state of lack.

Practicing gratitude helped me relax and feel calmer, so my energy changed, along with my luck. Within a few days, out of the blue, I got a call from an old friend who had the perfect long-term project for me. Tom also connected with an old business partner who wanted to collaborate again. Suddenly, the slump was over and we were rolling again, with no lasting damage.

While having work again was a huge relief, I realize that living through that frightening time was a real gift. I now have more empathy for the stress that my parents struggled with, trying to raise four kids on very little. I understand the kind of pressure that can lead to fighting, addiction, and divorce. I gained compassion for the burden of anxiety and depression that many people carry all the time.

The best thing I got from that tough time was my gratitude practice. It's a habit that colors my life every day. You hear about the "power of positive thinking" and that you should "look on the bright side," but what does that really mean? Finding the silver lining in the dark clouds is just a nice theory until you can find a way to actually bring it into your life.

I always thought that positive thinking was forcing yourself to see things in a way that wasn't natural. In my experience, people see the negative more easily than the positive. Practicing gratitude showed me the power of positivity and how to make it a natural part of every day.

While gratitude flows from your heart, the choice to open yourself to the feeling starts in your head.

Gratitude taught me that stress and every other feeling is a choice. Before this period in my life, I had never consciously chosen to feel gratitude every day, so I didn't know it would change my whole perspective.

What I'm most grateful for is the simple, astounding gift of life itself. The realization that we are all miracles, not just on the day we are born, but every day of our precious lives. We are all connected by this ineffable gift.

With this knowledge I have increasingly become a joyous person, bringing a grateful outlook to my entire life, rather than just the few moments a day when I'm actively practicing gratitude. It's made me feel like an incredibly lucky person again.

Practice

Practicing gratitude is easy and fun, a celebration, so approach it with a sense of lightness. It's okay to be grateful for a great pair of shoes or that attractive person you met today. Try each of these exercises a couple of times and then adapt them to your own style. Play with different patterns to find what feels right to you. The rest of the book builds on these basic practices and gives you others to try.

•   **Start with calm.** Start with this calming exercise to feel less anxious, so you can be open to gratitude. Take a few moments first to sit and get quiet. Breathe gently and slowly. Concentrate on your breath. Now, say this phrase (or something like it — find what feels right to you):

> **Today I am okay.**
> **Right this minute I have what I need.**
> **All is well. All is well.**
> **All shall be well.**

- **In the morning.** When you wake up in the morning, take a few minutes to focus on just your breath. Think of one to three things that you feel grateful for. Inhale gratitude, and savor the feeling on the exhale. Simply sit with the feeling of gratitude — allow yourself to really feel it.

- **At night.** When you go to bed each night, repeat the morning exercise, breathing in gratitude. It takes a while to get used to focusing on just one thing. Keep at it while you set all your other thoughts aside.

- **Give yourself a gift.** Give yourself a few minutes during the day. This can be while you're walking to lunch, in the elevator, walking the dog, or even in the shower or the bathroom at work. Think about one thing you're grateful for today. Concentrate on it and feel it.

ONCE YOU OPEN THE DOOR TO GRATITUDE,
LET ITS POSITIVE ENERGY SURROUND YOU AND
LIFT YOU UP EVERY DAY.

EVERY VICTORY COUNTS

Around Boulder, Colorado, almost everyone knows about Davis Phinney and Connie Carpenter Phinney. In a city that worships athletes and outdoor sports, they are both legendary cyclists.

In his book, *The Happiness of Pursuit,* Davis shares stories about his athletic career and his life since he retired from sports. In the book, he explains that "'Pursuit' … means taking responsibility for your own happiness." Davis' strategy for happiness is to celebrate every victory, large and small.

Every photo of his cycling wins shows his signature look — arms up in victory at the finish line, celebrating the moment. When Davis retired from racing, he began working as a TV commentator. He was a world-class athlete, but he noticed during interviews that the microphone in his hand kept shaking, and he often felt fatigued. After years of these and other mysterious symptoms, Davis was diagnosed with young-onset Parkinson's disease (PD) at age 40, and eventually had to give up his TV career.

Davis and Connie started the Davis Phinney Foundation (DPF) for Parkinson's a few years later. In addition to their multitude of race wins and Olympic medals, Connie and Davis are now legendary leaders of the Parkinson's "Tribe."

According to Davis, "Our focus is about improving the lives of people living with Parkinson's today. That focus stems from the fact that while there is no known cure for PD, many of our

Parkinson's Tribe are still simply waiting for the cure. But in my view, waiting is too passive a response: as you wait, you decline. I and numerous others in the Tribe live by example; getting up, getting out and pushing back against the inertia that PD imposes."

The Davis Phinney Foundation teaches exercise, self-care, and positivity. Their motto is: Every Victory Counts®. At Victory Summit® symposia, the DPF gathers local PD communities and their caregivers at no cost to inform, inspire, and directly connect them to available resources and to each other. Davis says, "These events are a rallying point for our often isolated Parkinson Tribe and emblematic of the type of work we do best." The DPF encourages the Tribe to celebrate all their wins, including: eating right, exercising, maintaining a positive attitude, and giving back to the community. At DPF events, Davis leads the group in celebrating victories, throwing up their arms in his classic "win" salute.

At an appreciation dinner for foundation supporters, Davis explained his philosophy: "When my daughter runs up to give me a hug, I don't have Parkinson's at that moment. I'm just living. If I can enjoy that moment, that's all I need. It's in those moments — where, if you are fully present, fully engaged in them, that no Parkinson's exists. Pure joy trumps PD every time! Moments of Victory = Moments of Cure. Make 'em count!"

Connie and Davis discovered that bike riding is great exercise for people with Parkinson's, and many of their Tribe have become serious cyclists. These folks and their supporters form the core of the DPF's Victory Crew, raising money and educating the public about this chronic disease.

My husband Tom is a high-school classmate of Davis. He and some other friends started riding several years ago in a DPF benefit ride called the Copper Triangle. The course covers three mountain passes in Colorado, and is challenging even for experienced athletes; they train for months to get in shape for it. Many Victory Crew members with Parkinson's tackle it every year, which is a testament to their determination to stay healthy despite the challenges of the disease.

Along with Davis, two members of this crew who inspire me are Carl Ames and Joe Williams.

Carl Ames is irrepressible. He regularly breaks into song on the road and "moos" at cows along the way. His nickname on the bike is "Bolt" because he takes off and leads the pack. He has turned his struggles into a way to help other people. He is involved as a fundraiser and volunteer for several Parkinson's organizations and runs his own non-profit called "Bikes and Basketballs for Kids." "I don't wish Parkinson's on anyone, but I wish everyone could have the opportunity to experience the things that I have experienced with Parkinson's, and more importantly, to experience the love, compassion, and generosity coming from wonderful family, friends, and strangers that I am able to experience these things with!" Carl was 46 when he found out he had Parkinson's and took up cycling to stay healthy and strong.

When Joe Williams was diagnosed, he was reluctant to share the news with his friends. But he decided that he could have an impact and use his diagnosis as a platform to raise money to help the Parkinson's community. He rallied his friends, who include former professional athletes, business colleagues, physical therapists, and fitness trainers to form the "Go, Joe,

Go" team. This close-knit team trains hard. Of course, the training keeps Joe and the whole team in great shape, but their other goal is to make significant contributions to the charities they sponsor. This group is fun to ride with, and they're known for their killer parties. Joe finds inspiration in this great group of people, and they are inspired by his caring, sense of fun, constant smile, and non-stop enthusiasm.

When I asked Joe to describe what "gratitude connection" means to him, he responded with one of his trademark poems:

Heart Song

For my ever growing tribe, by Joe Williams

To see another struggle,
To give to that other,
Whatever makes it immeasurably better
Makes my resolve stronger.

I ride with my tribe,
We ride together

Our struggle continues
We ride as we decline

We remain strong
In hearts and mind

To others we salute
And laughing, across the finish line, our horns we toot!
A joke we share, far from the truth.

> We step away from hours in the saddle,
> Our bottoms weary and our faces long
> We have pedaled so many hours
> The day too long
>
> We step away from our bikes,
> Our gritted smiles say not a word about the miles
> We fall into our loved ones' arms
> For each of you who cannot ride
> We step away, for you we ride...

Joe, Carl, and Davis deal with Parkinson's disease every day. But you'd never know it when they're riding. They glide along despite whatever challenges they face.

When Tom and his friends got to know Carl, Joe, and the rest of the Tribe at the Copper Triangle, they were inspired to do something big. They created the Friends for Phinney team and organized a 3,000 mile, cross-country benefit bike ride in 2013 to raise money for the DPF and visit Parkinson's groups across the U.S. (See friendsforphinney.org.) At each Parkinson's event, they donated a copy of the DPF's "Every Victory Counts" manual that explains techniques for living well with Parkinson's.

Carl, Joe, and other people with Parkinson's joined the team, riding at various times on this grueling trek across the continent. Carl chose to ride his first "century" (100 miles) over Wolf Creek Pass with the team in Colorado. Carl told me about that day: "Tom and the rest of the team really gave me the boost I needed to get up and over Wolf Creek Pass so that I could really celebrate and sing as we were coming on down the other side!"

Joe joined the team in Colorado and again in Pennsylvania, arriving in Pittsburgh after over 100 miles of riding. The days that Carl and Joe joined the team were some of the longest and steepest rides on the schedule. Those rides were huge victories, but they were made up of the small physical, mental, and emotional victories along the way.

Large or small, these victories make up the quality of our lives. Davis, Carl, and Joe exemplify the gratitude connection. They live in pursuit of happiness through focusing on service to others and celebrating every victory.

 Practice

The Davis Phinney Foundation's Living Well Challenge gives Tribe members a mission that we would all do well to live by:

- **Define Victory.** Do one thing that will make you feel better, function better, and enjoy life more.
- **Be Connected.** You are not alone. Connect with friends, family, your community, your partner. Reach out to support others and when you need support. Celebrate others' victories as your own.
- **Be Active.** The more you move, the better you will feel. Find an activity you enjoy and invite a friend, find a class, a gym, or get moving outside.
- **Be engaged.** Set concrete goals and get the support you need to meet them
- **Be Courageous.** Believe in yourself and your ability to effect change. Keep learning. Make the commitment to keep learning, live fully, and make every victory count.

Here are a couple more from me:

- **Be Grateful.** Celebrate every victory. Throw your hands up when you finish a run, a great bike ride, writing a chapter, cooking dinner, balancing the books, or any accomplishment, large or small.
- **Focus on Strengths.** Emphasize what you have rather than what you lack. When you focus on your strengths, perceived weaknesses diminish in comparison.

LOVE AND APPRECIATION

Every artist dips his brush in his own soul,
and paints his own nature into his pictures.
~Henry Ward Beecher

When you're at a museum and you admire the paintings, it doesn't necessarily mean you want to take them home to hang on your wall. You might love the colors and appreciate the skill it took to make them, but that's different from the feeling you get when you want to own a piece of art and see it every day. The artwork that you do want to take home grabs your heart or makes you happy.

I was at a three-woman art show opening where I got to see this in action. The show was a big hit, and the gallery was packed. I was there all evening helping out, so I got to walk around and see how people reacted to the work of all three artists.

With Cathy's multimedia work, I would see people tilt their heads, look more closely, step back, and nod. I could tell that people were trying to figure out how they were made.

When they got to Julia's work, people relaxed; their shoulders moved downward, and their scowls went smooth. People related to the soothing nature themes in her pieces.

And when people got to Jenny's art, they visibly reacted. Some just stopped, some backed up. Many put a hand to their hearts.

Jenny's work is abstract, with bright colors and swirling movement. It has some indescribable soul that reaches out to you. I saw people over and over have a visceral response to her work.

When I asked about Jenny's art, most people couldn't say why they liked a piece, but they had to have it — now. I felt the same way. All her pieces sold that night, including the one I'm looking at as I write this.

That's the difference between appreciation and gratitude. Gratitude is more than just appreciation. With gratitude, love is an essential element. It's not just intellectual, it's a heart connection.

Practice

You can just stay in your head when you think about gratitude. You can simply appreciate, in an intellectual way. But the grace comes in feeling it.

When you're thinking of things you're grateful for, try putting your hand over your heart to connect to a deeper feeling.

LIVING THE GRATEFUL LIFE

Your gratitude practice is just that: a practice, a habit. It's not something you have to sit down and do for 20 minutes a day, it is an easy practice that sneaks into all the nooks and crannies of your life. I didn't know this when I started, but practicing gratitude makes you happy. Gratitude is a high-energy emotion, and once you start feeling it, it seeps into everything, like air.

Pretty soon, it becomes a lifestyle, and changes you in subtle ways. Like you'll smile at someone you think is judgmental. You might wake up in a good mood instead of dreading the morning. You might shake off the anger about your commute and look forward to your evening with the family.

One way to practice gratitude is to replace the habits in your life that just don't serve to make you happier, clearer, less stressed, or more peaceful.

It's hard to just stop a bad habit. Trying to "not do" something all the time feels bad, as if you're just waiting to feel guilty if you slip up. Much better to replace an old habit with a new one.

Here are a few ideas to help switch out some habits that are no longer working for ones that can help you.

Old Habit

Panic first thing in the morning: "Oh, no! I'm late, gotta rush, too much to do, where's my stuff, I should have…"

Grumpy morning person: "Don't talk to me until I get my coffee! You know I'm not a morning person. I hate perky people. I'll feel better after a shower…"

Negative self-talk: I'm so stupid! Nice work, doofus. What an idiot! I should have known better…

Criticism, gossip, or judgment: "She shouldn't wear such short skirts." "He's so handsome, I bet he cheats."

Come in the door complaining: "You should have seen the traffic!" Somebody cut me off! My boss is a jerk, I hate my job!" Constant complaining makes for an unhappy existence. And it makes other people want to run away.

Ending the day angry or upset. Going to bed in a bad mood sets the tone for your dreams and your next day.

New Practice

Morning Gratitude Practice: Wake up 15 minutes early so you can relax in bed before you get up. Focus on three things you're grateful for.

(See above): After you do your morning gratitude practice for a few days, see if you feel a little more cheery when you get up. (This one thing proves the power of gratitude.)

Self-love: React to your mistakes like you would if your best friend goofed. Show some compassion toward yourself. Mistakes are human. Forgive yourself and move on. (See Love Starts Here)

Humor: When I start getting "judgy," I see a cartoon judge (black robes, white wig) in my head and say, "here comes the judge!" Laugh at yourself and you'll lighten up about other people. Find something constructive and kind to contribute; it will change your perception.

Focus outward: Before you start your rant, consider the people you're with. "Hi, nice to see you. What's going on with you?" When you focus on someone else, the rant is not the first thing on your mind. If you do still need to get something off your chest, ask first. "I've got something on my mind. Can I talk to you about it?"

Evening Gratitude Practice: Just like the morning practice, focus on three gratitudes for a few minutes before you go to sleep.

MAKE SOMEONE HAPPY

When I walk into Joan's house, she throws her hands up over her head and squeals, "Amy!" with a huge smile. It's the greatest feeling to be greeted like that. I can't help but know that I'm loved and appreciated. I see her light just beaming at me, and I can't help but beam right back, throw my arms up and hug her. Welcome someone you love with this kind of enthusiasm, a way that truly expresses your love, appreciation, and excitement. It might feel silly or over the top at first. If this isn't your normal style, it will have even more impact. Just have some fun with it.

THANKS

There is hardly a sweeter word in any language than "thanks." Any way you say "thank you" is a positive way to connect with other people.

- Share something you appreciate about someone instead of keeping it to yourself. Comment on a pretty dress, a great haircut, a fabulous smile. Send a text to your friends to say hello or send your thanks. It will make their day and yours.

- A real, heartfelt, handwritten thank-you card takes a bit more effort than a text or a phone call, but it can have more impact — it's unexpected. One way to make this easy is to carry thank you cards with you. A couple of cards in your car or bag or desk drawer allows you be spontaneous.

- Give people cards in person or leave them anonymously. Give them to people you know and love, and to people you'll never see again.

- If you don't have a card, thank people anyway. Share a text or an e-mail. Give someone a hug or a sticky note or write a note on your business card. I keep a stack of business cards that have "Thanks!" printed on the back. That way I can write a quick note to someone I appreciate.

- Surprise your partner with a fun note tucked into a wallet, purse, car, mirror, or lunchbox. Spontaneous love and appreciation keeps things fresh in your relationship.
- Thank the children in your life for doing the chores, drawing a picture, or for doing some kind thing, or for just being who they are.
- Make up for lost time. It's never too late to say "thanks." Reach out to people you admire and just let them know how they have affected your life and how you appreciate them. Even if a person has passed on, you can write how you feel in a journal so you acknowledge that person's impact.
- Start your day with a "thank you" message. Whether you're at work or home, think of someone from the day before who impacted you in a positive way and let that person know. It takes just a couple of minutes and sets the tone for the rest of your day.

RECEIVE GRACIOUSLY

When someone thanks you for something, you reply.... (Please choose the best answer)

1. Oh, it was nothing
2. Just doin' my job
3. Aww, shucks, anybody would have done the same thing
4. Forget about it!
5. You're welcome

The obvious answer is "you're welcome." But how many times do we answer with one of the others?

"Thank you" is a gift. Not accepting thanks is like throwing that gift back or stomping it under your heel. Maybe you really feel that you did nothing and you don't deserve a thank you. But the person thanking you feels differently and wants to connect with you through gratitude. Accepting thanks graciously invites more grace into your life.

BLESSING
Try this blessing or create your own:

> *I begin my day in gratitude for the love and beauty in my life. I seek peace and healing. May I be filled with the positive power of Spirit.*

VISUALIZATIONS
These visualizations take very little time. Try these and make up your own.

- Imagine a person or a group of people surrounded by a beautiful, white light. The power of this light keeps the negative at bay. Try doing this at the start of a meeting and see if you think it makes a difference in your attitude or in the way people interact.
- Breathe deeply for a few moments, and as you exhale, imagine any negative or dark energy in yourself returning to the earth through your feet.

SCOOP IT UP AND LET IT GO

"If I could help you increase your happiness in two minutes or less, would you want to try it?" I got a big "yes!" from the crowd, so I invited everybody to stand up and Scoop with me.

The Scoop really broke the ice and got people smiling, laughing, and connecting. When I asked, "Did it work? Are you at least a little bit happier?" I got another loud "Yes!"

Now I want to teach it to you, but first, a little background. I learned The Scoop from my husband, Tom. It's an essential part of my gratitude practice, because it puts gratitude into action. Here's the story of the scoop in Tom's words:

> "This gentleman named Matt, a friendly young guy about 6 foot 6, came up to the car at the recycling center and greeted me. He said, "You gotta do something with me today."
>
> I said, "Well, what's that?" Matt said, "You gotta learn The Scoop."
>
> I said, "I'm game!" It was a perfect morning, beautiful sunshine, and this guy's energy was crazy big.
>
> So I hopped out of my car and got ready to do The Scoop.
>
> Matt shared this story with me. He has a brother that he rarely gets together with. But they used to go skiing a lot. They started their ski day on the mountain with The Scoop.

They would get off the chairlift, plant their skis in the snow, look at each other and say, "We're gonna have the best day ever." They did The Scoop with three intentions for their day: let's be safe, let's be happy and let's celebrate this day of being together."

Then he taught me The Scoop.

Matt said, "Get your stance, and stand tall with your feet apart. Take your hands and turn them up to the sky. Think of your three intentions for the day.

For your first intention, with palms in front of you, reach up over your head, sweep your arms out on either side like you're scooping up a giant snowball, and bring your arms up in front of you again.

For your second intention, do another big Scoop.

For your third intention, make it the biggest Scoop you can, and hold the energy of all three scoops in your hands, like you're holding a chalice.

We're gonna take those scoops with all their power, and throw the energy of those Scoops up into the sky and expect many, many blessings to come down on us."

The Scoop is a celebration. Feel the energy after you release it to the sky!"

You can tell Tom loves The Scoop. He teaches everybody he knows to Scoop. Each person does The Scoop a little differently. You get to change it up and make it your own.

Of course, I make it The Scoop of Gratitude, so my intentions are three things that I'm grateful for, and then I send that gratitude energy out to the world. I imagine that a little of that positive power sprinkles down on me and the people I'm with, and the rest floats out on the breeze.

If you'd like to see The Scoop in action, please visit The Gratitude Connection channel on YouTube.com.

Practice

- **Scoop it up and let it go.** Try the Scoop and see how it feels.
- **Share The Scoop.** Spread it around – teach The Scoop and you'll see what fun it is to do together.
- **Hug someone.** A Scoop is always better when you end with a hug.
- **Scoop at home.** A lot of people have adopted The Scoop as a family ritual. Carl and his family scoop to celebrate holidays, accomplishments, to thank someone – they scoop for any reason at all. Spencer and his family make it a part of any gathering they have, and they Scoop every day on the beach on vacation. Try teaching it to your family and see how it takes off!
- **Scoop at work.** At his conference one day, late in the afternoon, John noticed people were glazing over after all day in their seats. It's a syndrome I call "death by PowerPoint." So he stopped his presentation and asked everybody to do The Scoop with him. These serious business people had to step out of their comfort zones and do something that looks a little silly. But they had fun (and woke up). And then they were thinking about gratitude. John says people are still talking about it months later. Try it when you need a boost of energy. Scoop to celebrate wins, big or small. Scoop when your group needs a shot of positive power.

THE POWER OF THE PAGE

Fill your paper with the breathings of your heart...
~William Wordsworth

Writing as a way to connect to your inner workings is nothing new. "Journaling" is such a common idea that we don't really think about what it means to sit down and write. What exactly do you write in your journal? How do you access whatever deep secrets are hiding in your psyche?

That's where Julia Cameron's book, *The Artist's Way,* comes in. Cameron developed the book as a "course in discovering and recovering your creative self." The most important part of this course is the commitment to writing every day.

The writing is personal, a way to work through whatever you're struggling with. The goal is to help you move beyond your blocks so you can discover the creative, expressive artist inside.

Cameron calls this writing "morning pages." The idea is to start writing early in the morning before your left brain has started to get busy telling you what to do. You just start writing whatever floats to the top of your mind.

Since nobody else is privy to this writing, some interesting things come out. Some are beautiful, and some are ugly and dark and pissed off. And — that's OK. Cameron explains it this way: "These daily morning meanderings are not meant to be art... Pages are meant to be, simply, the act of moving the hand across the page and writing down whatever comes to mind. Nothing is too petty, too silly, too stupid, or too weird to be included."

Morning pages are a safe place to celebrate your victories or to rage and vent, to get it out and learn whatever it has to teach you.

Sometimes the words flow easily and quickly, and other times it's a chore. But when you make it a routine, your subconscious mind knows that it has a place to process some things that you've been hiding from yourself.

I'm often surprised by the powerful memories that come up in my morning pages and impressed by my own power of denial. For example, sometimes old memories come up, and I realize I've never looked at how I feel about them. And bam! Those emotions hit right then. How could I have avoided feeling that for so long? But there it is, I can feel it and see the effects right now. And I usually get some new insight. Then I can move ahead and see the gifts in that experience.

This kind of writing can become a part of your gratitude practice. There's something very powerful about putting words on paper. It can help you get past whatever is blocking your happiness, and can free you to move forward.

Practice

Here are a few things to try:

- When you wake up, set aside a few minutes to jot down whatever you're grateful for.
- If that doesn't come easily, ask "what do I need to write today?" You might be surprised by what comes up. Write it down.
- Give yourself permission to write whatever comes up. No censoring, it's OK. Even if it feels scary when you're writing it, the issue could be blocking your path to gratitude and happiness. Getting it down on paper takes the mystery and secrecy out of it. Like most things, it may not be as scary in the daylight.
- Your writing may bring up old anger, grief, and memories. Welcome them. If you wonder why they're showing up now, go ahead and ask the pages. "Why now?" "What do I have to learn from this?" "How can I let it go?" Then listen. Write down the answers that come to you.
- At the end of your writing sessions, turn your focus back to gratitude. Write down whatever pops into your head.

You can write every day, or as often as you like. Do what works for you.

WORRY = LOVE?

If you don't worry about people you love, does it mean you don't care?

Your parents probably worried about you as a kid — I know mine did. They are both world-class worriers, so I learned from the best. I remember being surrounded by the power of my mom's worry. It seemed like a force of nature.

When I was a teenager, I had the rare opportunity to travel to Russia. My mother was supportive in every way, sending me off on what she knew was the trip of a lifetime. Months after I returned (safe and sound), I found out that she had been so sick with worry that she spent most of the time I was gone in bed. So, while I was still flying high from my wonderful experience abroad, I knew that her life had been hellish during that time, and she was still recovering from the stress. Did I cause that? Should I have stayed home? I felt responsible, but I also knew that she loved me so much that she couldn't stand to have anything happen to me.

The result of her worry was that she got sick, but I think she also felt that the energy of her worry somehow kept me safe.

Parents worry about their kids, but may not understand how their worry affects their children. How did your parent's fear and worry affect you as a kid? Do you keep things from your loved ones so they don't worry?

When people worry about us, we can get messages such as:

- You're not safe
- You're not smart enough to take care of yourself
- Other people are evil and out to get you
- You're not good enough
- No one loves you like I do — look how much I worry about you!
- You are vulnerable
- You should be frightened
- Only I can take care of you
- Worry means love
- You should worry about me and others you love
- My worry protects you from bad things

Practice

You can transform your perspective from feeling the worry that was sent your way to connecting to the love behind it.

Look at this in your own life. Were your parents worriers? How has that affected you? Would you have thought you weren't loved if your parents didn't worry about you?

How does the worry you learned as a child affect your life today?

How would you change this cycle with your own family?

Visualization

If you're worried about the people you love, the worry probably starts with you. Someone has worried about you, so you learned that there is plenty to be worried about.

Here's a visualization to free yourself of the worry energy that has been directed your way:

Make yourself comfortable in a quiet room. Breathe deeply and feel yourself relax.

Now breathe that feeling down through your body.

Picture yourself in a garden, with a warm and inviting pool nearby. As you move toward the pool, you feel yourself carrying a weight of all the negative thoughts and worry that has surrounded you since you were born, and even before.

See the steps that lead down into the pool of clear warm water, fed by a hot spring. On the first step, as your feet touch the water, you feel a swirling. You look down and notice the worry energy moving from your body into the water. Notice what color it is.

As you continue to move into the water, you feel lighter and lighter, as the water takes the worry from your body, taking even the deep-seated worry energy from deep within.

The water washes away into a stream and drains the worry with it, far away from you. As the water washes away the worry, send a blessing along with it. Bless all the people who worried for you, worrying as a way of loving you.

Relax and rest in the pool for as long as you like. Revel in the feeling.

When you're ready, slowly leave the pool and come back to the world.

Reflection

What did you feel in the pool?

Who did you think about?

What do you take with you from this experience?

FROM WORRY TO PEACE

As an adult, I brought the "worry is love" philosophy to my relationships. I dated men who were involved in risky sports like skydiving, hang gliding, and rock climbing. That was a perfect outlet for my worry! Putting the "worry" into a relationship right away is an instant recipe for codependency. It meant that I could place all my energy into worrying about their safety, so I didn't concentrate on my own life. No wonder those relationships didn't flourish.

My husband, Tom, is not such a daredevil, but I still worried about how he might get hurt — driving, biking, or playing sports. And it wasn't just in my marriage — I was incredibly stressed from worry about everything from my family to my job to my ailing dog.

But I did catch myself, and knew that it was damaging me and all my relationships.

I found *Feel the Fear and Do It Anyway,* a simple and powerful book by Susan J. Jeffers. It's about how to face your fears. I'm not talking about the rational fear you feel in a dangerous situation. I mean the fears that live only in your mind — spinning around until they become a part of your everyday life, diminishing your joy bit by bit.

The concepts in that book helped me take over my life and let go of my biggest worry. I had an irrational fear that my husband would die. That fear was present in my mind at all times.

In the book, Jeffers encourages you to really examine your worst fears. She has you walk the path of your worry to its conclusion, and feel it. What would result if the worst did actually happen? Would it hurt so much you can't imagine it? Yes. Could you survive even the worst thing you're afraid of? In most cases, the answer is yes.

It comes down to the fact that you can handle most anything that comes your way. Hopefully you won't have to, but the fact remains that you would feel deep pain. And, you'd get up the next day and do it again. Wow. "I can handle it" is the basic message. It's simple and empowering.

I realized that if I could handle that fear, I could handle anything. My worry was misplaced energy that could be going toward something more positive. It helped me change my behavior from telling my husband in the morning, "Have a safe day, be careful!" To "I love you, have some fun today!" It meant I could start from love and have a fun day, too.

That alone is amazing. The energy I used to spend on constant worry is transformed. I was able to give up a debilitating and damaging habit overnight.

When you change any habit, it's a good idea to replace it with another (better) habit, or you might slip back into it.

Meditation is my main method, so I chose to turn the scary scenarios of my worry into a platform for transformation.

In meditation, I picture my husband when he's happy, on his bicycle, when he is filled with what makes him whole. I focus on seeing him that way and how it feels. I breathe out gratitude and love toward him, surrounding him with light and lifting him up in joy. This practice makes me so happy that I easily slip into seeing myself and my whole world in the same light and love. The more I practice, the less I worry. And the energy of fear dissipates and becomes peace.

Meditation

Please enjoy this meditation as a first step to transforming worry to peace. Listen to this mediation online at: *http://www.amycollette.com/do-you-have-a-worry-habit/*

Today we're going to focus on changing the energy of worry into peace — for ourselves and for those we worry about.

We begin with a special blessing for you to easily let go of your worry. To gently embrace the gifts of transformation. To gracefully receive divine guidance and the peace that comes with it.

Close your eyes and take a deep breath and relax as you exhale.

And again, deeply breathe in, and breathe out any tension.

One more deep breath in, and slowly exhale.

Find your own gentle rhythm, and feel yourself relax more deeply. Let the muscles in your face relax.

Now breathe that feeling down through your body.

As you exhale, breathe out through your heart. Your heart energy begins to fill the room, surrounding you with love and comfort. You are safe and supported.

In your mind, picture the person you worry about most. It's someone you love deeply — it might even be you.

Now, picture that person in their happiest moment.

Breathe out your heart energy, surrounding your loved one with love and light.

How does this picture make you feel?

Breathe in this feeling, letting it fill you up. Breathe it in, integrating it deep into your body.

With gratitude, accept the divine gift of this feeling.

Concentrate again on your breathing. And as you gently come back to the present, take this gift with you. Remember that you can access it at any time. You can easily transform worry into peace.

FOCUS ON THE LIGHT

The first thing you do when you walk into your house at night is switch on the light so you can see. It's unnerving to knock around in the dark.

But we tend to focus on the dark and the negative in our heads. I think it's a natural human tendency to fixate on the negative because it's a survival mechanism. It probably comes from our caveman days when we were hunted by animals and had to constantly be on guard for danger. It's an instinctual habit that's hard to break.

Another example is when you're hurting. You know how you can't stop feeling the space that's left when you get a tooth pulled? Or when you scrape your knee, your whole body seems to hurt? When you're hurt, all your energy is focused on that pain.

The same thing happens when you're getting annoyed with someone. All you can focus on is "Stop that, you're driving me crazy!"

How about when someone you love is hurting? You can drive yourself nuts trying to figure out how to help, how you could have prevented it, and wondering why it had to happen.

But what if all your precious energy was going toward love and healing rather than focusing on the pain and worry?

A health scare taught me to change my focus from obsessing about worst-case scenarios. I had to wait a couple of weeks for test results from my doctor, who said there was a slight possibility I could have cancer. You can guess what my brain did. Instead of focusing on the fact that the doctor said "slight chance," my brain heard "CANCER" and stuck there. I intuitively knew I was healthy, but my brain was telling my body to freak out. My stomach was in knots and my spine was like a concrete pillar.

It turned out my intuition was right. The test results were negative for cancer. So all my stress over the possible outcome was wasted energy.

Practice

I confided my worries to my friend Betsy, and she taught me this beautiful practice to focus on the light rather than fixate on the darkness.

Stand with your feet shoulder width apart. Plant your feet solidly, and feel them rooted to the ground. Get as comfortable as you can: Soften your knees, relax your shoulders and let your arms hang easily by your sides. Close your eyes if you like.

Take three deep breaths. Feel the air in your lungs. Feel the oxygen flow through your body, renewing you with every breath. Allow yourself to relax more as you continue to breathe.

Now, visualize a bright orb of light above your head. It gently shines down on you. It is light in every sense of the word. Move your attention to the light. How does the light feel? Absorb that feeling and let it settle in your heart, let it flow through your body all the way to your feet.

Ask the light to help remind you to focus on it when your mind chooses the negative.

Take a deep breath in and thank the light as you exhale.

Take a few more deep breaths and open your eyes.

That light is your highest, most noble self. It's a natural part of you and is always there to help you shift and refocus. What a gift!

After you've done this practice a few times, it starts to become a regular habit to focus up and into gratitude.

May your perspective be light.

CORNUCOPIA

On Saturday mornings when I was a kid, the race was on. Which one of us would wake up first, fly down the stairs and claim the prize?

My brothers and I played the cereal game every weekend. Mom and Dad slept in, so the competition could be wicked. Whoever won the race to the kitchen got to the sugar cereal first. So not only was the winner guaranteed a big bowl of the tooth-decaying stuff, but also the plastic toy or prize in the box. Whoever showed up late got the leftovers.

This game was just kids having fun, but the competition speaks to our ancestral human fear of not having enough food to go around. (Although I hesitate to call sugar cereal food…) When we were cavemen, we didn't know where the next meal was coming from.

This primal fear of lack is a factor in why so many of us have issues with weight and food. Some people eat for comfort when they're worried or stressed. Others are the opposite.

When I'm feeling stressed, I tend to not eat enough. It seems like a distraction when I should be getting something done! It's just another way of seeing lack instead of plenty: there's not enough time to do everything and take care of myself.

An abundance mentality means that you intuitively know that there is more than enough of everything. Appreciating food and developing healthy eating habits are ways that you can start seeing abundance immediately.

Practice

These practices help you incorporate food into your gratitude practice, as well as nourish your body and soul.

BEFORE AND DURING MEALS

Many spiritual and religious practices teach giving thanks before meals. It's a good time to combine your gratitude practice with a new sense of abundance.

Give thanks. As you sit down to eat, open your eyes and heart to all that went into putting that food on your table. In spoken or silent prayer, give thanks for:

- The land that grew the food
- The hands that nurtured and harvested it
- The people who prepared your food
- The colors, flavors, and variety
- The ethnic traditions it came from
- The people who are sharing your table

Share your thanks. You can give thanks silently any time, but you can also involve others around the table. Invite people at the table to share their gratitude.

Focus on eating. A study published in the American Journal of Clinical Nutrition shows that people eat less and enjoy the food more when they are not distracted, and they tend to snack less after meals. Put away the phones and devices and focus just on eating and enjoying other people at the table.

Eat only until you're full. As you begin to eat, savor the first bite and relax into enjoying the food in front of you. As you continue to eat, notice how your body feels. At some point, you reach a point where your body is full enough — satisfied.

AFTER EATING

Awareness. Now that you've had just enough, take a moment to sit back and relax. Notice how your body feels; satisfied, but not stuffed. This is the sense of taking care of yourself, loving yourself well.

Share your abundance. Focus on taking that sense of fullness into the world — so you can contribute in a bigger way to your work, your family, community, a creative project, or a new business idea.

BREAK THE MOLD

After Keith was diagnosed with a brain tumor, he had to take a serious look at how he was living his life, running his business, and raising his kids. He considered all those nights and weekends away from his family while he was working hard to build his business. He thought about the notion that he needed bigger and better things all the time. Even though he was very smart about money, he still spent more than he made, with no end to this pattern in sight. For years, in the back of his mind, he had wanted to live his passion: to teach people about how they could start living their dreams now. No more waiting to retire to follow their souls' calling. But first, he had to follow his own advice. Keith's health crisis was the catalyst for writing his book and becoming a speaker and consultant. Keith is healthy again and doing the work he is passionate about.

"Pretirement" is a term Keith Weber coined in his book *Rethinking Retirement: How to Create the Life You Want Without Waiting to Retire.* The word means challenging our preconceptions about abundance, work, and "the way things are." Keith is a successful financial advisor who once had these preconceptions, or myths, as he calls them: work hard, save, and invest enough money, and someday, maybe, you'll have enough to retire. Then, if you're still healthy and have the energy, you can do the things you love, like travel, be creative, start a business, have fun, and enjoy your family.

His book is a mix of financial guidelines and personal coaching to help people discover and finance their dreams. I know his formula works, because I used it to make a plan to leave the corporate world and follow my own path.

In our culture, success usually means material success, money, the way things look to other people, job titles, cars, homes, kids' educations, and on and on. But we should be able to define success and happiness for ourselves.

The exercises below can help you uncover your myths and create your own path to abundance.

What is your first memory about money?

How does that memory make you feel? How does it affect how you deal with money now?

What are your money, success, and abundance myths? Write down the sayings, thoughts, fears, or ideas about money you grew up with. (For example, "money doesn't grow on trees.")

1.

2.

3.

4.

5.

6.

7.

8.

9.

10.

Circle the ones you still believe.

How are these preconceptions working in your life now?

What's on your list to do when:

- You have time

- You have enough money

What's your dream?

Now dig deeper. What's the really big dream that you're holding back? The one you're afraid of even writing down? Come on, you can dream big…

Practice

What resources (talent, skills, experience, wisdom, money, material things) do you already have to start making your dream real?

Bring those parts of yourself into your gratitude practice. Focus gratitude on your unique self and what you bring to the world.

What more do you need?

How can you be more effective at managing your finances?

Try feeling grateful in advance for those things that you need to realize your dreams. Take a moment to write or draw a picture of it and experience how it will feel.

FORMULA FOR SUCCESS

Now and then it's good to pause in our pursuit
of happiness and just be happy.
~Guillaume Apollinaire

The myths we talked about in the previous chapter make up the conventional formula for success. Work hard, be successful, and that will make you happy, right?

But what happens when we reach a goal that we've set? We are happy — for a moment. Then that accomplishment just becomes the new normal, and we're back to feeling like we usually do and striving for the next "success."

Shawn Achor says that we ought to try the formula the other way around: that happiness could make us more successful. And he has the science to back him up. His books, *The Happiness Advantage and Before Happiness,* cite numerous studies that prove his point.

Achor studies what he calls "outliers," those people who do not fit into the "normal" plot curve. In other words, these people are "off the charts." Most studies would eliminate the data from those folks because they don't fit in. But Achor studies them to find out what makes them extraordinary.

He found that the happiest people make the most successful people, too. His studies show that people who assess themselves as happy have:

- Superior productivity
- Less burnout
- Lower stress
- Greater sales

Achor suggests that we should focus more energy on learning how to be happy. By looking through a lens of happiness, our definitions of success and how we get there would change.

I like Shawn Achor's work because he's a funny and entertaining guy, but also because one of his top three ways to become happy is: practicing gratitude!

The happiness that Achor and I are talking about is not a fleeting, jump-up-and-down kind of happy, but a foundation that is always there, no matter what is going on. Of course, things happen that make us angry or sad, but that solid foundation will be there under our feet.

The way I built this foundation was with gratitude. Happiness was available all along, but I had to go looking for it, and practicing gratitude helped me find it. It was like when I was learning to play guitar – I could play a couple of chords, but that didn't mean I was making music. I had to keep working at it every day.

Once I started practicing gratitude, it became like muscle memory, like changing chords on a guitar. It's just a part of who I am, and it takes no effort now, it's become automatic.

Practice

To make the connection between happiness and abundance, I tried some ways to change my perspective (and my myths) about money. Try these practices to find out what works for you:

- **Think like a pirate.** Try thinking of your money and investments as treasure. I use an antique trunk to store all my financial files. It's a visual reminder that my "treasure" is hidden in there.

- **Build wealth.** With all the baggage we carry around about money, maybe we need a different word. You're not "saving money," you're "building wealth."

- **Fill 'er up.** We can get stuck in always thinking about our lack of money rather than appreciating what we have. When you get a check, try thinking about how it fills up your account, rather than on what you still can't afford.

- **Thanks!** Take a moment before you start to pay bills to give thanks for the ability to pay them. Focus on the value you get from the products and services you're paying for.

- **Spark someone else's abundance.** Anonymously leave dollar bills in random places, like on a grocery store shelf, in a newspaper, or in the pocket of a jacket at the thrift store. Pay for the next person in line at the coffee shop. Donate to a cause you believe in.

- **Dance break.** Put together an abundance playlist of fun "money" music that you can play when you need to lighten up about money. Get up and move to the music. Have some fun!

You can get the idea from a few of the songs on my list:

- Billionaire (featuring Bruno Mars), *Travie McCoy*
- Best Day of My Life, *American Authors*
- You and I, *Ingrid Michaelson, Busbee, Trent Dabbs*
- If I Had A Million Dollars, *Barenaked Ladies*

CAN YOUR HAPPINESS WAIT?

Everyone in Melinda's small town knew her smile and how she always remembered their favorite coffee drinks. Scott says he has a coffee maker in his office down the street that he never used. He would much rather get out of the office and get a shot of "Melinda energy" with his coffee.

Melinda loved her customers but was feeling that she just had to move on and do something else. She was frustrated with the company and the lack of benefits. She had reached the top of the pay scale, so she didn't see any opportunities there. She needed a change but couldn't see what to do next.

She signed up for a seminar about discovering your life purpose and your spiritual path. She was hoping for some insight into what she should do.

During the seminar, the teacher picked Melinda out of hundreds of people in the audience to come up and talk with him on stage. Although she really didn't want to be in the spotlight, Melinda went up the stairs and joined him.

"Are you doing what you came here to do?" he asked her. She smiled and said, "I don't think so, that's why I'm here."

"What do you do for work?"

Melinda said, "I run a coffee shop."

He studied her, quiet for a moment. He said, "You're like a bartender in the movies. People tell you their stories, you're the shoulder they cry on."

When she smiled in acknowledgment, he said, "So all day, you connect with people, and you give them a blessing in a cup."
Without hesitation she said, "Yes."

He said, "In this work, you profoundly affect people every day. It's what you are meant to do right now. You will do that until it's time to do something else."

The teacher could intuitively see right through her, what she meant to her customers, and what they meant to her. Behind her eyes he could see her kindness, playfulness, and generosity. He was saying that the work Melinda did was part of her path because she loves connecting with people. He was asking her to feel grateful for that positive part of her work.

With that said, her job still didn't give her all the things she needed, such as benefits and better pay. Melinda decided to go back to school to get her degree in social work, so she could continue to connect with people and make a difference in their lives. In the meantime, she continued to run the coffee shop and enjoy her community as she worked toward her dream.

Practice

The challenge is that you always hear, "Do what you love. Follow your passion." But that can seem so vague and far off if you're not sure what your calling is. Even if you know exactly what it is that you want to do, it's probably going to take a while.

In the meantime, maybe you can find a way to see your current work in a different way, and use that clarity to move forward.

- Research shows that having just one good friend at work increases your happiness. Do you have a friend or positive relationships at work?

- What do you enjoy about your work?

- What attracted you to this work in the first place?

- What have you learned?

- How does your work allow you to serve others?

- Can you see how your current work is part of your path or expresses an essential part of you?

- Can you see a way that it might lead to your next step?

SACRED SPACE

"Where do you go to rest and rejuvenate?" When I asked Jill this question, she laughed and said she hadn't had a vacation in years.

"I mean at home. Is there a place you can go to recharge, meditate, or just have some time to yourself?"

When she answered, I could hear that she was starting to get teary. With a nervous laugh she said, "No one in my house would leave me alone that long. If the kids aren't asking for something, the phone's ringing and Jerry needs something for a client. I never get any down time until I'm sleeping." As she thought about it, she said, "I do make time for phone sessions with you once a week. I try to schedule it when the kids are at school and Jerry's in a meeting."

That was a start. At least Jill had carved out an hour to herself. During this session, we did a guided visualization together. I invite you to come along:

Visualization

Get comfortable, sitting or lying down in a quiet room. Close your eyes, breathe, and let your body relax. Release any tension you're holding in your body. Fall more deeply into the cushions, and put all your worries and thoughts in a basket by the door.

In your mind, picture a secret garden, a place that is special to you. As your eyes adjust to the garden, walk around and see what's there. Somewhere in the garden is a sacred place all set up for you. Look around to find it.

When you find that place, settle in and get comfortable. Relax into it — this is your safe haven.

Now, simply ask the question: "What do I need today?"

Let the wisdom come. Take a few moments to listen and understand.

When you are ready, come back to the room, bringing with you a sense of gratitude for the gifts you received today. Gently open your eyes and stretch. Know that you can return to the garden at any time.

After the visualization, Jill got a feeling for what it was like to open her heart to receive. She needed the time and space to experience that state, and she wanted to do it regularly.

Practice

The important thing about sacred space is not the place or the things in it, but how you feel in that space. A ritual of creating the space helps you find what makes you feel peaceful, calm, happy and whole. When you know how that feels, you can access that feeling anytime you like.

Here are some ideas to help you carve out some sacred time and space for yourself. Try the ones that resonate with you, and maybe even some that scare you. Dare to create this for yourself.

- **Plan it.** Schedule some time every week to yourself.

- **Carve out a space.** Maybe you want to create an altar where you can go to light a candle, get quiet, and meditate. Or maybe you have a whole room where you can shut the door and escape. Even a place outdoors can be your special place.

- **Wake up early.** My friend Michelle gets up at 5:00 am every day to write and meditate before her kids wake up.

- **Escape at lunch time.** Sit in a park, close your office door, or even sit in your car.

- **Take some time after work.** Schedule some "me" time after work and before you go home. An hour at the coffee shop or on a hike can help you "decompress" from work before you reconnect at home.

- **After the kids go to bed.** Laurie's ritual is taking a bath (sometimes with a glass of wine) after the kids go to bed. Everyone knows this is her special time — no one bothers Mommy. Her husband gets some time to himself then, too.

Now try creating some time to connect with yourself more often — what if you could have this every day?

LOVE STARTS HERE

One day in a gift shop *A Little Book of Prosperity Magic* by Cynthia Killion jumped off the shelf at me. I probably liked it because it has "magic" in the title. It's a book of rituals to help you understand abundance as just another form of energy in your life.

One of the most compelling is the "I love me" ritual. We tend to be so hard on ourselves, so the purpose of this exercise is to turn our inner critic off and replace it with love and appreciation. Killion instructs you to say "I love me" or some form of that phrase for ten minutes. I read that and felt myself squirming inside. "That's stupid!" I said to myself, thinking that ten minutes was a long time to keep that up. But discomfort is usually a loud and clear signal that I need to pay attention. If I'm fighting it that much, it's either really bad or really good for me in terms of transformation. Since I thought it couldn't do any harm, I decided to try it on a long drive by myself.

I got to a point in the drive that was straight and long. I turned off the radio, glanced at my face in the rear-view mirror, and started. "I love you." That felt a little weird and I giggled, feeling silly. I tried another tack. "I love me!" "I love myself." "I love Amy." I looked at the clock and it had only been about a minute. Nine more minutes of this? It was agonizing and I was still resisting it, but I kept at it. Pretty soon I was shouting the words, trying to have some fun with it. It still felt a little strange, but something started to happen. It was a subtle shift in perspective. I began to see myself outside of my usual critical view. I started to really feel a love and appreciation for myself that I usually reserve for the most special people in my life. I know that they have a spark of the Divine within — we all do. This exercise helped me connect to that spark inside myself. It was amazing.

I really didn't think it would work. But it's a case of "fake it 'till you make it." I started out faking it and ended up seeing the value of the exercise and the value in myself.

There is an aspect of forgiveness to this practice, too. We can be pretty tough on ourselves, holding back love because of some bad decisions in the past. This practice helps you break down those barriers and connect to your heart. Once you start feeling genuine love, it's easier to let those judgments go.

Practice

Improving your self-talk and learning to love yourself is a powerful way to banish the negative in your life.

I LOVE ME EXERCISE

Now it's your turn to do the "I Love Me" exercise. Here are some suggestions to try.

Set aside some time when you will be uninterrupted. It's important to focus just on you.

- Be in your sacred space
- Open your heart and mind to whatever comes to you during this "love time" for yourself
- Open up enough time to complete the 10-minute "I love me" ritual and then have some time to yourself afterward
- Commit to the full 10 minutes before you start

- Say it — try saying "I love me" different ways, then try the same one several times in a row: I love me, I love myself, I love (name), I love myself!
- Notice your feelings
- What feels different about each phrase?
- Try picturing yourself as a newborn baby — you were a brand new miracle (and you still are)
- Say "I love you" to yourself as a newborn, and at different times in your life
- How did you feel after five minutes?
- How did you feel after 10 minutes?
- Let "I love me" become a mantra — something that is so natural that it's like a living prayer

I AM WORTHY EXERCISE
This exercise is taken from Nancy Rynes' book, *Awakenings From the Light.* In this exercise, look in a mirror and say:

"You are worthy. You are special. You are a miracle!"

After you're comfortable with that phrase, try it this way:

"I am worthy. I am special. I am a miracle!"

An easy way to make this exercise a daily practice is to post the phrases on your mirror to remind you.

BACK TO THE FUTURE
Write a letter from your future self to your current self. Project yourself 10, 20, or 30 years into the future and write a letter from the perspective of that distance of time. What will your future self thank you for? What are you doing now that your future self will look back on with admiration and respect? Have some fun with this. You can make a time capsule with this letter, or put a reminder in your digital calendar every year to review it and write a new letter.

Top Ten List

The next step is to look inside and list the top ten things that you like about yourself and integrate them into your gratitude practice.

1.

2.

3.

4.

5.

6.

7.

8.

9.

10.

THE POWER OF LOVE

When you say "I love you" for the first time, you're scared to death that your beloved will not say it back to you or feel the same way. We're so conditioned to be careful about when and how we say those words. That caution really means that we want control over other peoples' feelings. We don't want to say it unless we're pretty sure the object of our affection will say it back. But think about it — even if your loved one doesn't say it back or doesn't feel that way, your feelings of love and appreciation are still the same.

In my family, it usually took a near-fatal accident or major surgery to break out the words "I love you." I grew up thinking that you would wear it out or it would become meaningless if you just threw around "I love you" all the time.

Fortunately, my husband feels differently. When we were first together, I thought it was just the blush of new love. But after a couple of decades, he still says "I love you" many times a day, and I'm in the habit, too.

Knowing that saying "I love you" doesn't "wear out" the feeling means that we always have more than enough love to share. When you say it, it reminds you of that feeling and nurtures your heart just like sunshine on a plant. And it can keep growing, given the proper nourishment.

Gratitude can open the door to love. I think about all the movies and books that start with one person despising the other one, but by the end of the story, they're in each other's arms, proclaiming their undying love. Take "The African Queen," the classic movie with Humphrey Bogart and Katherine Hepburn. As the heavy drinking boat captain (Bogart) and the prissy missionary (Hepburn) get to know each other, they begin to admire and appreciate each other's strengths. Together they fight the enemy, the river, the weather, and the wild critters, and end up in love.

Practice

To be able to give love unconditionally, fill yourself up with it, starting with loving yourself. When you are filled to overflowing, love energy flows naturally from you. (See the previous chapter: Love Starts Here.)

- **Be brave, be bold.** Go ahead and say it first. One way to relieve your anxiety is to preface those beautiful words with something like, "I want to tell you what's in my heart. There's no need to say or do anything but just relax and receive this right now." Then, take a deep breath, feel it, and say it. What a gift.
- **Start with gratitude.** When you're struggling with a relationship, in an argument, or just annoyed with someone, try to get a different perspective. Think back on something that you admire or respect about her. Consider a time when you felt grateful for something he did or said. When you're less upset, maybe you can even open the door to reconciliation with one of those memories and get back to saying "I love you."
- **Say it often.** Surprise your family and friends by coming out with "I love you" more often. You'll feel more comfortable with it the more you do it, and they will too.

---

* I'm not advocating that you push your affection on someone who doesn't welcome it. If your feelings are not reciprocated and make the other person uncomfortable, please respect that.

PERFECT DAY

On a hike one day, my friend told me that she'd just had the perfect day. She said that she had signed up a new client, had lunch with an old friend, went running with her dog, and then had dinner with her family, which her husband cooked. That was her idea of a perfect day.

Then I had to think about what my perfect day would be. I've had a lot of the elements of a perfect day, just not all on the same day.

But then I thought — a perfect day could look a lot of different ways. So, I started looking for parts of a perfect day every day. Some possible elements of a perfect day:

- **Waking up happy:** by yourself or with the person you love
- **Connecting with friends and family:** by sharing a meal, a quick coffee, a hug, a phone call
- **Connecting with yourself:** through meditation, exercise, quiet time, reading, writing, singing, etc.
- **Connecting with nature:** with a walk by the creek, a visit with a pet, watching a hawk soar
- **Moving your body:** hiking, biking, skiing, dancing
- **Healthy habits:** eating healthy food, nourishing yourself, self-care
- **Doing good work:** by serving your clients, partners, co-workers, employees, boss, and charitable organizations
- **Getting great sleep:** by making the bedroom a sacred space, safe and comforting

Practice

What elements would make up your perfect day?

How many of those elements happened today?

Celebrate! Feel the gratitude and share it!

How can you help more of those things happen tomorrow?

Instead of waiting for them all to happen on the same day —
practice looking for the things that make you happy today.

EXPECT THE BEST

Happiness is having a large, loving,
caring, close-knit family - in another city.
~George Burns

Jeff's sister, Wendy, called on the Tuesday before Thanksgiving
and said, "It would be really nice if you could come for
Thanksgiving since dad has been so sick this year. We'd love
to see you when we're not all in a hospital room." So Jeff got on
the first available plane to Dallas and then got a cab to Wendy's
house. His mom was there too, so they all had dinner together.
It had been a long day, and Jeff was looking forward to falling
into bed soon. He turned to his sister and said, "So, Wendy, am
I staying with you or Mom?"

When Wendy looked down at her lap, he turned with a grin to
his mom. "I guess it's you, then, huh?"

"Jeff, I'm so sorry. I've got your uncle staying with me right now.
Randy's home from college and staying at Wendy's."

After a tiny pause, Jeff realized that he was going to have to find
a hotel room. In a daze, he finished his meal and got another
cab. He took the driver's recommendation on where to stay. He
never thought he'd rush to Dallas on his family's request and
end up with no place to stay. Jeff was upset and fighting a lot
of old feelings of rejection and humiliation.

It wasn't the first time something like this had happened, and
probably wouldn't be the last. Jeff stayed for Thanksgiving and
made an excuse to head back to Denver as soon as he could.

Jeff knew the rejection scenario could easily happen again the next time, so he had to be prepared. He had options, including not going for another visit anytime soon. Which he definitely considered. But he decided he didn't want to stay away forever, so he made a plan to surprise his mom for her birthday in May.

First, he rented a car and booked a room near his parents' house. This way he avoided the possibility that no one would have room for him. Staying at the hotel also gave him the privacy he never got when he stayed with family.

That night in his hotel room, Jeff made a list of all the things he loved and appreciated about his parents and his sister. The things they did that made him laugh and the times when they had helped him.

Before he went to the birthday party, he felt his chest getting tight with anxiety. Jeff wanted to celebrate with his mother, but he remembered past gatherings that ended with hurt feelings and somebody storming out (usually him). He thought, why would this time be any different?

But Jeff decided to expect something different from himself and his family this time. He wanted some kind of healing. He didn't know how it was going to happen, but Jeff decided to forgive his family for how they had hurt him in the past, hoping that he could start fresh.

That choice changed his perspective from dreading the worst to expecting the best. It shifted his focus back to the birthday girl, where it belonged.

He went shopping at a local store where they knew his mother. He asked them to put a special gift together, and it helped get him get into the spirit of celebrating another birthday with her.

Jeff went to the party and had a great time surprising his mother. He had taken care of all the things that would trigger his stress: transportation, lodging, and a gift. He set up everything he needed, and knew he could escape at any time if things got weird. He made loving decisions and took good care of himself. Jeff also approached the gathering with healing in mind, and had his gratitude list to remind him of the things he loved about each member of his family. This trip was the most peaceful family gathering he could remember.

Practice

In your relationships:

- **Create a gratitude list.** Before a family gathering, spend some time alone and make a gratitude list. Write down things you love about each person. Take a moment to feel the love and appreciation you have for them. Then, take the list with you to refer to when people start driving you crazy. It can help to remind you why you love them (and save your sanity). Make a gratitude list for yourself, too – things you love about yourself.

- **Express your gratitude.** When you see a person who usually pushes your buttons, start the conversation with something on your gratitude list. "Remember when you taught me that dance in high school? That was really fun. It meant a lot to me that you'd take the time with me. Thank you." Notice the energy change within you and in that relationship.

- **Find compassion for the behavior that bugs you.** How can you love or laugh at that aspect rather than letting it drive you crazy? For example, I know a guy who repeats everything he says. I used to just tune him out because that habit made me crazy. But he does have interesting things to say. So to keep myself sane, I count the number of times he repeats every point. I make it a game and it keeps me listening.
- **Imagine healing.** Maybe you've never considered that your family relationships could be healthy. Picture what a healed relationship would feel like.

Expect the best at work with:
- **Difficult coworkers.** You know, the ones you'd rather run away from? Give a compliment to that person you struggle with. Make it genuine, and really try to find something positive about that person to comment on.
- **Meetings.** Is there a way you can bring a little humor to a boring or contentious meeting? Instead of diving right into the agenda, try greeting everyone in the meeting and "checking in" first with how their day is going.
- **Projects.** It's easy to get stuck doing the same things the same way. Try brainstorming: write down even silly ideas just to get it all out of your head and onto paper or a white board. Then look for patterns or connections you didn't see before.

THE POWER OF COMPASSION

When Roxanne found out her father was terminally ill, she called me. "I've got to deal with this stuff with my dad."

Every time we talked, she poured out the frustration, anger, and resentment she had toward him. "Everybody thinks he's such a great guy," she said. "But would a great guy treat his own daughter this way?" When I asked about her history with him, it seemed to always go back to the same incident. "There were seven of us. I know that's a lot of kids to keep track of, but he forgot me. He just drove off with the rest of them in the car and left me standing there." Roxanne was so hurt and upset that she was shaking. "I'll never forget the feeling I had right then; that he just didn't care. I could die for all he cared. I can't stand the feeling of hating my father, but I still do."

The power of her emotions was overwhelming. This incident had taken on so much significance that it affected her ability to trust people.

I suggested we do a visualization together. I started by having her settle into a comfortable position, and we did three deep breaths together to relax. When I could sense that she was ready, we began.

"Picture a stage in front of you. You're in some kind of theater, sitting in the audience, looking up at the stage. The heavy velvet curtains are closed. When you're ready, the curtains open. What do you see?"

"I'm in a big room with my brothers. It smells funny and has a bunch of chairs."

"Where are you?" I asked.

"At the hospital."

"Why are you there?"

"Mom is sick. We came to visit her. But they wouldn't let us younger kids in to see her. You have to be twelve and I was only eight." Her voice trailed off.

"What else?" I asked.

"Well, I guess dad had to bring us all because there was no one to watch us. We have to stay in the waiting room with a nurse. She says she doesn't get paid to babysit a bunch of brats. She's going into mom's room now, and dad and my two oldest brothers come out. Dad says it's time to go home."

"What next?"

Roxanne is quiet for a moment.

"I'm looking out the glass doors. I'm scared."

"Tell me what else you see."

"Dad's car is pulling up fast." After a bit Roxanne continues. "Dad is getting out of the car. He looks kind of crazy. He's yelling my name. I'm standing inside, wondering why he can't see me. He keeps yelling, looking around outside. Finally, he sees me and runs inside."

Roxanne got quiet then, except for a couple of sniffles. She continued, "He gets down on his knees and he's hugging me hard. I just stand there. I feel stupid, and he's acting crazy."

She sounds annoyed now.

"Is he saying anything?" I asked.

"He's saying something, but I can't hear him," Roxanne said. "It's OK. Just look away for a minute and take a deep breath. When you're ready, look back at him."

"Oh, God. He's crying. He's actually crying!" With a choked voice, she said, "He's saying, `I'm so sorry, baby girl. I'm so, so sorry. I was so scared. I thought someone took you. But you're OK, you're OK, everything's OK. Momma's gonna be alright, too, baby. We're all gonna be OK.'"

Roxanne got quiet again. I asked, "What next?"

"I'm just quiet."

"OK," I said. "When you're ready, the curtains on the stage close. Take a deep breath and come back to this room."

When Roxanne opened her eyes, she looked exhausted. "What's sticking with me is the look in his eyes when he hugged me. He looked at me like I was the most precious thing in the world, and he was never so relieved in his life. I never knew he felt that way about me."

"All I ever remembered before was standing there feeling lost. I didn't remember that mom was sick, and that he was taking care of everything at home then. He was worried about mom and trying to juggle all of us kids with no help."

"So how do you feel about it now?" I asked.

"Well, I can see it from his point of view. He was overwhelmed. And I was a very quiet kid. I didn't run outside when I saw he was leaving. Maybe I was testing to see if he'd notice I was missing. As a kid who wasn't getting enough attention, I was making it about me." She grimaced, feeling guilty.

"Sounds about right for an eight-year-old," I said.

Roxanne smiled. "I've seen that look in my dad's eyes recently. I guess I thought that he was trying to make up for leaving me that day. But now I think he's always really felt that way about me, I just couldn't see it."

Roxanne was able to reconcile with her dad and even thank him for his love.

She was able to break down her defenses and connect with him as an adult rather than feeling that separation as a hurt little girl.

Practice

In our work together, Roxanne started a process that would lead her to deeper healing. We talked about how she could continue to connect with herself and her feelings for her dad. Together, we came up with these exercises:

Forgiveness

Roxanne had turned the anger she had toward her dad into beating herself up for blaming him and for wasting so much of her life hating him. How could she get over it? Forgiving him came easily when she connected to compassion for what he was going through back then. So the next step was finding compassion for herself.

We all have that little kid who got hurt still inside. It's our responsibility and our privilege as adults to nurture and console that little kid. As loving adults, it's our job to now raise that kid right:

- **Start the conversation.** In a quiet moment, close your eyes and ask the child inside to talk. You can start the conversation. Try something like, "I love you. I'm here to make sure you are always safe and happy. I will always love and take care of you." Listen for an answer or simply a sense of how the child inside is feeling.
- **Check in.** Every once in a while, check in with that child inside — especially when you're nervous or scared. Reassure that child that you are doing your best, making good decisions and taking care of business. Let your child know not to worry.
- **Have you hugged your inner kid today?** Roxanne found that she got great comfort from visualizing her little eight-year-old cradled in her lap.

Forgiveness can open the door to gratitude. Although she struggled with it at first, Roxanne started spending a few moments of her gratitude practice each day focusing on feeling:

- Gratitude that her path led her to compassion for her dad
- Gratitude for a renewed connection with him
- Gratitude for the healing that it brought to both of them

Where are the places in your life where you've made a decision about something based on how you felt as a child?

Try going back to one of those moments in your mind. Can you understand how you were feeling and why? Can you empathize with what others around you were feeling then?

Is there a gift of knowledge or understanding for you?

LIFE IS DANCE

I think of dance as a metaphor for life. Dance can be joyous and light, skipping around with your arms up or embracing your partner. It can be fast and happy, like a polka, or slow and sexy like a tango.

Dance can also be melancholy and sad. One of the most touching dances I ever saw was performed by a Russian ballet company. On stage were just two men. One was dressed all in red, the other in white. As they moved together and apart, they told a story of war and death. It was tragic and beautiful. It may be the only time that ballet brought me to tears.

Life is like that. It's not always happy, but the sad parts can teach you something about yourself, and help you to love other people and let them go.

Practicing gratitude helps me understand and appreciate all these phases.

Practice

Create a metaphor of your own. Does "Life is dance" work for you?
Or is it more like:

- Life is play
- Life is a hike in the woods
- Life is a day at the beach
- Life is sailing
- Life is art
- Life is family

What's your unique way of seeing life?

Use this metaphor to celebrate the good times. Let it remind you
of the flow of Spirit in your life.

COUNTING UP

When my father-in-law died, my friend Doug shared some wisdom he learned when he lost his own father. His dad had been so sick that the family thought they might lose him immediately. But he pulled through emergency surgery and recovered. Doug said, "At that point I realized that every extra day was a bonus. Not just for him, but for my mom and the rest of the family. After five months he passed away. Those five months made me think about the 'bonus time.' That means we're counting up every day, not counting down to the end. I hope my story helps a bit."

It did help then, when we were grieving, and it still helps give me a different perspective. I try to remember that each day with people I love really is a bonus. Rather than marking that day off the calendar as one less than I had yesterday, I'm counting up each day as one more.

It's easy to feel grateful for the happy times, like falling in love or enjoying your family. But what about when you lose that person? That's when the strength and power of gratitude can really sustain you.

When you have built a foundation of seeing your life through the eyes of gratitude, you can move slowly and sadly through these times and still have the core of gratitude holding you up, flowing through you all the time. It helps carry you to a different understanding of grief and how you can survive it.

How can you find gratitude in a time of loss? You can focus on:

- Gratitude that your loved one was part of your life
- What you learned and how you grew through them
- How you shared your heart and your wisdom
- How you allowed yourself to be vulnerable enough to love them and yourself
- How that person is a part of your journey, your spiritual path

This is a gift for your gratitude practice; another way of seeing the world. May you see each day as a bonus and remember to always count up.

Practice

Using the metaphor you created in the previous section (Life is Dance), revisit a painful loss in your past.

- Is there another way you can look at it with your new metaphor?

- Is there something more you can learn from it?

- Is there a way for you to see any gifts or blessings in it? Can you feel gratitude for those gifts?

If you can't yet, give it some time. Look back on this loss from time to time and see what else you can learn from it.

Look at every day in your life and the lives of those you love as a bonus – as an extra, something to celebrate.

GOOD GUARD DOG!

One day my doorbell rang and Keetna went to work. She barked her head off, jumping up and down, looking at me and then back at the door. I went to the door and saw a nervous-looking woman standing there. It was Julie, a new neighbor from down the street. I told Keetna, "good guard dog," and petted her head to calm her down.

As I opened the door, Julie stepped back off the front stoop. She looked shaken and said, "Is your dog a Rottweiler?" I laughed and explained that my little black Lab was friendly but loud.

Keetna did her job that day, warning and protecting me, which she took very seriously. It was my job to assess the situation and decide if I was safe or if I was potentially in danger.

I think of my ego as my internal guard dog. After trying for years to fight my ego from blocking my way, now I see it as my early warning system. Its job is to go crazy barking to warn and protect me, but ultimately I get to make the decisions about how to respond.

I used to think that I needed to totally reject or eliminate my ego — that it was all bad and I didn't need it.

But you want your ego to do its job, just not to make the big decisions. Eliminating your ego would be like tossing out your sense of touch — your body's defense mechanism to let you know if something is going to burn you.

Since it's kind of a fun way of looking at it, the guard dog metaphor keeps me smiling at my defense mechanism, not taking it too seriously. I stay connected to my ego through gratitude, and reward it for doing a good job.

For example, it seems that every time I have a chunk of time set aside to work on my writing, my stomach starts getting tight, I feel a little sleepy, or I get an invitation to do something else. I know that's my ego jumping up, telling me it's better to be safe than sorry. It's pretty scary to think I can write a book and put myself "out there" in the path of potential doom, right? But after receiving that warning, I get to decide. I smile, take a deep breath, say "good guard dog!" and keep writing.

At other times I've let my ego make the decisions and regretted it. In a work situation I was denied a promotion when I failed to claim my own work and let another person take the credit. In another instance, I kept my mouth shut about someone's drinking problem and abusive behavior. By listening to my ego telling me I would lose my job if I spoke out about it, I enabled her dysfunction and kept myself in a miserable position. In both cases, the people involved were my supervisors. I feared that I would "make them look bad" as well as possibly get myself fired. I was taking responsibility for them (which was not my business) and not taking loving care of myself.

My ego was doing what it does — warning and protecting me against possible bad outcomes. I based my actions on that fear rather than on what was healthy and loving for me. These situations kept coming into my life until I could wake up to how dangerous it is to let fear overpower my intuition and better judgment.

Reflection

How does your ego affect your decisions?

How does your ego help you?

Describe any situations where you could encourage and thank your ego for protecting you.

How can you be more active in realizing that your ego is at work?

HAPPY OR SAFE?

At one point I was feeling particularly stuck, unable to move to the next level of my business. It seemed like I was sabotaging my own progress, scared to take it to the next level.

So I stopped for a minute, imagined that guard dog that is my ego, and asked, "Don't you want me to be happy?"

The answer shocked me. "No. I want you to be safe."

That is the essence of the ego — it's about keeping us safe, not making us happy. That conflict between where we want to go and the powerful pull of safety is where we get stuck and unable to overcome our inertia.

The word itself seems neutral. It sounds like inertia just sits there, not going anywhere. But really it's a powerful force in our lives because it takes a huge amount of energy to get it moving, like pushing a car uphill.

Inertia is the state your ego would like you to stay in — it's safe to be parked where you are instead of moving toward the unknown. What if there are hills or rocks in the road? What other dangers might be waiting around the corner? Your guard dog would prefer you stay in one place so he can keep a close eye on you!

It helps to keep a visual like this in mind when you feel stuck. Then you can thank your vigilant guard dog, but still get off the couch and get moving, even if it does upset the dog...

Practice

- Connect with the positive aspects of your ego by finding a powerful visual that works for you. Maybe the guard dog metaphor works, or you think of your ego as a Roman soldier or a tiger or a protective guardian angel. Get a picture of this totem and open the conversation.

- Take a few quiet moments to sit and connect with your ego when you're not in conflict with it. See your ego totem in your hands and surround it with the light of compassion. Ask for a deep understanding of the needs that motivate it.

- When you can find that compassion, let gratitude come in. Breathe out gratitude toward your ego totem, deeply feeling the love that you have for an entity that has your best interest in mind always.

- Now ask it to have compassion for you, too. Feel your strength and say thank you for the warning. Make it clear that you, and not your ego, will make the decisions.

You might just decide you'd rather be happy than safe.

LEAD THE DANCE

Lou was a beautiful ballroom dancer, and an even better dance instructor. In everyday life, he looked like he was carrying the world on his shoulders: a little hunched over, head hanging down, and eyes cast toward the floor.

But when the music started, he stepped out on the dance floor. He reached his full height, his shoulders were straight, his head was high, and his smile was beautiful.

He would hold out his hand for me to join him. He would start twirling me around the floor as if he was light as air. That joy and ease transferred to me as his student. I picked up on his love of dance and how it could shift his attitude, his entire demeanor. He always said that dancing is easy. "Here, just watch me do it a couple of times."

Sometimes he'd spin off, pretending that he was holding a partner in his arms, but dancing by himself. I liked just watching him dance. Then, he would swing by, sweep me up and suddenly I was doing the steps with him. It *was* easy and it was joyful. Through dancing I learned that Lou was a great leader because he showed me how to do something and then expected me to emulate it. Then he expected me to teach others to do the same. That's what good leaders do. Pretty soon I was teaching dance, too.

Since dance is my metaphor for life, I've had to learn to not be afraid of leading the dance. For me that means spreading the word about the positive power of gratitude. I invite you to embrace your passion, and then to be bold enough to lead others to it.

Reflection

When you are passionate and happy about something, it shows. So just by doing what gives you bliss, you're contributing your light to the world. Other people may find your energy irresistible. I mean, they might want to have what you have, feel like you do, shine as brightly.

- What makes you "light up," like Lou does with dance?

- Are you doing enough of it? Do you feel satisfied? If so, celebrate!

- If you want to do more of it, how can you find the space in your life for it?

- How can you share it?

CONTROLLING THE CHAOS

My idea of housework is to sweep the room with a glance.
~Erma Bombeck

When I walked into Bina's office, I had to force myself not to gasp at the mess. I'm used to a few piles on a desk, but her piles were impressive. On top of filing cabinets, book shelves, the floor, chairs — everywhere you looked were piles of books and papers, some several feet high.

She smiled when she saw me squelch a reaction. "I know where everything is," she said calmly. "Really?" was all I could get out, still trying to wrap my head around the mess. "Try me," she said.

Bina is a tax accountant, so I said, "OK. Say I need to file back taxes for three years ago. Where can I get the 1040 book for that year?"

Bina got up and walked to one of the piles, lifted about half of it up, retrieved the book and handed it to me with a grin. "Told ya."

Bina really does know where everything is, but her style of organizing would drive most of us crazy. Just the thought of walking into that chaos every day makes me feel drained.

For most of us, the clutter in our physical space reflects some chaos in our heads. A messy home or office can also be an energy drain, providing an excuse to stay stuck.

What's your clutter? Piles of magazines you're going to read "someday," the kids' toys, dirty laundry? Knickknacks covering every surface?

Clutter and chaos can drain your energy because the need to clean it up is always on your mind. When stuff takes over your space, it means that you don't have room for anyone or anything else to come in. Bina had to move a pile off of a chair if more than one other person came to her office. It made me wonder if the mess put off potential clients. Would she have a bigger business if she had more space to grow it?

Bina wouldn't agree that controlling the chaos gives you peace of mind. But if you do, here are some things to try:

Practice

If it's time for you to get organized, try these:
- **Clear your desk.** File it, recycle it, or put it on your list.
- **Make room.** Do you have room in your space to invite people in? Maybe you're embarrassed by the clutter, or there's no room for people to sit. If so, divide the work into small bits. Don't attempt to clean the whole place at once. I suggest you start with your personal spaces, like your bedroom to make space for yourself first. Hopefully having a clutter-free space to sleep in will motivate you to tackle the public places (like the living room) next. Now that you have space, you can share it.
- **Increase your peace.** What's the area that drives you crazy if it's messy? For some it's the kitchen sink, others it's the living room floor or the bathroom counters. Whatever it is for

you, make sure that area is clean before you go to bed. It's great to start the day facing a clean place rather than the mess you dread.

- **Thank yourself.** When you face a clean space, thank yourself for making the effort. Add this small moment to your gratitude practice.

LIGHT AND SHADOW

By now you know I like to focus on the positive. But I know there are powerful lessons to be learned from the "shadow" too. You wouldn't be the person you are today without your shadow and the tough experiences you've been through.

Debbie Ford overcame incredible challenges before she became a well-known self-help guru. In her book *The Dark Side of the Light Chasers,* Ford describes how she had to decide at one point in her life to leave the darkness of addiction and walk toward the light of recovery and self-love. Finding a way to love and accept the dark side of herself was an integral part of her path to the light.

We may not have addictions to face, but we all have some traumatic experiences and memories. We can go along most days without having to face them, but it takes some energy to keep them suppressed. The memories are there, waiting until we're ready to shine a light on them. We're afraid that they'll have some power over us, and they do. Because the effort of keeping all those memories hidden steals a little bit of our energy every day.

Our shadows live in the basement, conveniently hidden. We have to make a special trip down there to see them, and most of the time we're happy just leaving them there, like boxes of old school stuff. But keeping all those shadows down there takes up space that we could use for something more productive.

The upside of going to the basement and turning on the lights is that our dark sides have something to teach us. But we have

to be willing to learn and brave enough to face them.
Here is what's in it for you:

- **Safety** — Those memories can't hurt you now; they're in the past (or they can be if you can let them go)
- **Clarity** — What happened or why it happened might look different to you after a few years have gone by
- **Forgiveness** — you have an opportunity to forgive yourself or someone else
- **Compassion** — When you can see a shadow more objectively, you might see that when you hurt someone or when someone hurt you it was not intentional
- **Lessons** — You could learn something new about a past experience

So, the challenge is to build up your light until you feel strong enough to go to the basement and face your shadows. Opening those old boxes in the basement may cause you some heartache initially, but you'll be surprised by the strength you have to handle them.

Visualization

What power can you reclaim from your old dark secrets? This visualization engages your intuition and imagination. Allow images and information to pop up in your mind as you do this exercise.

Get comfortable and quiet in a place that you feel safe and protected. Close your eyes and breathe deeply. Feel yourself relax.

Now breathe that feeling down through your body. Feel the strength that's within you. Whatever you have to face is in your past; you have already lived through it. It has no more power to hurt you.

Open the door to the basement and take a look around. Before you go down the stairs, take a deep breath. As you exhale, breathe out through your heart. Your heart energy begins to fill the room with light. You are fully surrounded and protected by the light. Descend the stairs until you are in the main room in the basement. You can see the room but cannot be harmed by anything in it.

There's a gift box in the room somewhere. Look around until you find it.

When you find it, open it. What gift for you is inside?

Take a moment to understand what it is and the message it has for you. If you don't understand, simply ask.

Breathe in the message to integrate it into your body. Thank the gift and the message.

When you're ready, open your eyes and come back to the present.

CHOOSING HAPPINESS

Kate is a successful business woman, but she struggles with staying positive. She told me once that the best thing parents could do for their children was teach them how to be happy. Her mother tended toward depression and her father was just a big kid. Her parents divorced and tried to find happiness on their own, but still struggled with the same issues.

"So, how am I supposed to be happy?" she asked. "If they couldn't figure it out, what makes me think I can?"

It's a dangerous road to travel — replaying the tapes from other people's lives even if they are our parents. Our culture tends to glamorize parenthood, sending the message that all our parents' energies should be directed toward their kids to create the most nurturing environment, the most loving atmosphere to grow up in.

But the reality is that our parents' energies were fractured by the competing demands of jobs, money pressure, relationships, their other kids, and their own aging parents. Many parents are just barely surviving, and keeping the kids clothed and fed is about all they can do.

As kids, we had to try to make sense of a world in which we didn't have all that information. We just thought that we should emulate our folks. So, like Kate, when we saw our parents being unhappy, we drew certain conclusions:

- People can't be happy
- Other people can be happy, but not my family
- My parents are unhappy because of (fill in the blank)
- I can't be happy if my parents weren't happy

Now it's time to reexamine those conclusions. There is a wise, loving adult within us who is the perfect person to help.

We have to make decisions every day, all day: what to eat, how to solve problems at work, if and when to exercise, who's going to pick up the kids, on and on. The everyday decisions can be pretty easy. But others can be almost immobilizing: whom to date or marry, where to live, how to handle our money, and how to care for our parents.

All those decisions add up to a happy or a hectic life; to satisfaction or feeling like you're running in circles. They can make the difference between doing what is loving for us and doing what we think we "should" do; putting everyone else's needs first.

Kate gets especially confused when she needs to make decisions about relationships and commitments. Not only was it difficult for her to think about a lifetime commitment like marriage, it can also be hard deciding about going on a trip with friends. She can get caught up in the logistics and trying to analyze other peoples' feelings. Will the timing work out? Will her friends be upset if she doesn't go?

When our brains starts spinning like this, we get stuck. You can probably relate to this kind of stress. It can make you feel like you can't make a decision or that it's easier to make no decision at all. But you have the power to decide what makes you happy.

When the spinning in your head starts, take a minute to relax and get quiet. Breathe deeply to calm down your heart rate and your spinning head and ask yourself, "What is the loving thing for me?" "What decision makes me feel happy?"

It really is that simple. As long as what you do does not harm other people, connecting to what is right for you is the only decision to make. Over time you'll get more comfortable making decisions based on this good judgment of what makes you happy. Taking responsibility for your own happiness breaks the cycle of modeling your happiness on what you grew up with.

Practice

Think of the times when getting clear on how you feel might help you make a decision about whether to commit to something:

- A family gathering (forget the "obligation" factor — what's loving for you?)
- An after-hours business event
- Meeting with an old friend
- Starting a new business
- Going on a first (or second or third...) date
- Committing to a relationship
- Going on a trip or vacation
- Taking a new job or project
- Doing business with a new person

This practice can help when you feel pressured, uncomfortable, or just "off" about a decision.

Ask yourself:

- Do I really want to do it, or do I think I "should" do it?

- When you think of following through on this decision, how do you feel? Notice your energy: do your shoulders slump with the weight of it or do you feel light?

- Would I do this if I didn't think I had to?

Be honest with the answer to the question: What is the most loving thing for me?

The more you do this practice, the more you can look back on your decisions with gratitude for taking care of yourself first. You might find that everyone else around you starts taking care of themselves, too.

What are some situations in your life where you can use this practice?

CLAIM YOUR POWER

How do you feel around people you think are really fantastic in some way? They're super smart, beautiful, successful, wealthy, and maybe even famous. How do you act around them?

I used to be a little star-struck and intimidated about being around such star wattage. These people come across as confident and comfortable. So why didn't I?

I was too busy comparing myself, and finding myself "less than." I could never "compete" with these superstars, so I went small. Going small for me means fading into the background, not saying much, becoming a wallflower at the edge of the action.

I was invited to an exclusive luncheon with high-powered people at a fancy restaurant, and I almost didn't go because I was intimidated by the glamorous guest list. I had to really fight the feeling that I wasn't "one of them" and that I didn't belong there.

I knew that this negativity was plain old fear, but the noise it created in my head was pretty loud. I decided to work through it and go to the luncheon anyway. I wore something colorful, gave myself a pep talk, and walked in the room as if I did this every day.

The people there were gracious and friendly, so I relaxed and the fear wore off in a few minutes. I had a great time.

And I got a special treat — a woman I really admired and had worked with years before was there. I immediately went up to her and re-introduced myself. She surprised me by being just as thrilled to see me as I was to see her. If I had decided to let myself be defeated by the chatter in my head, I would not have had that wonderful connection.

When you "go small" by deciding that you're not good enough, you're showing up as a different person than you really are. You are unique in the world — no one has your sense of humor, your experience and insight. What are you missing out on by not being who you are? And what is the world missing from you? You might not know until you decide to love and appreciate yourself enough to "go big" and claim the power within you.

Practice

Emulate your superhero. Think of a person you know who really has it together — someone who is successful, fun to be around, and full of easy confidence. That kind of person is just like you, but claims his or her power, and shows up big. That's what makes people magnetic — the kind of people you feel drawn to. What makes her or him special? What are some qualities that you can emulate?

Claim your power. This is a simple three-step process you can do in a few quick minutes before you walk into a potentially scary or stressful situation. It helps you shake off the anxiety and find your core of strength.

Plan to arrive early so you can have a few minutes to yourself before you go in. You can do this in your car, in the bathroom, backstage, or wherever you are.

1. **Shake it off.** Take a cue from our dog friends and shake the nervous energy out of your body. You can just shake your hands if you like, or you can jump up and down, shake your head, and move all that energy out of your body. If you feel a bit silly, all the better. It might make you laugh and feel lighter.
2. **Breathe it out.** Take a deep breath in and blow out any tension left in your body.
3. **Breathe in calm.** Place one hand on your solar plexus and one over your heart — whatever feels soothing. Take a deep breath in, filling your lungs with calm. Gently exhale and repeat at least two more times. Feel the calm in your body and the strength it gives you.

Now you are ready. Enjoy.

READS AND RESOURCES

All of these books have inspired me. I hope that you find magic and inspiration in them.

- *A Little Book of Prosperity Magic*, Cynthia Killion
- *The Artist's Way*, Julia Cameron
- *Awakenings from Spirit*, Nancy Rynes
- *Before Happiness*, Shawn Achor
- *Creative Visualization*, Shakti Gawain
- *The Dark Side of the Light Chasers*, Debbie Ford
- *Feel the Fear and Do It Anyway*, Susan Jeffers
- *The Happiness Advantage*, Shawn Achor
- *Rethinking Retirement*, Keith Weber
- *The Spirit Tree*, Marilee Ross

SONGS

See The Gratitude Connection channel on YouTube.com to play this list of songs. You'll also find videos on how to do "The Scoop," and other gratitude and happiness resources. Copyright laws prohibit me from sharing the lyrics of these songs, but I provide this list so that you can seek them out if you choose.

Blessed

Closer To Free

I Can See Clearly Now

Why Worry

Take My Love With You

Hall Of Fame

Church

All Star

Be What You Are

Home

Love God and Everybody Else

If I Could Change the World

Best Day of My Life

Sweet Forgiveness

She Just Wants to Dance

Thankful

Little Star

Happy

Do You Love Me

Shadow Days

Shooting Star

Worthy Of

ABOUT THE AUTHOR

Amy is a best-selling author and award-winning speaker. She has always been a spiritual seeker and self-help junkie, finally settling on gratitude as her spiritual practice of choice. When she's not writing, Amy likes to speak to groups, teach workshops, coach, and enjoy life with her husband, Tom.

Connect with Amy at amycollette.com.

AmyCollette.com

embrace the postive power of thanks

25697089R00073

Made in the USA
San Bernardino, CA
09 November 2015